HUGH LATIMER

An Introduction

James Alsop

ELSP

Published in 2011 by
ELSP
11 Regents Place
Bradford on Avon
Wiltshire   BA15 1ED

Origination by Ex Libris Press
Bradford on Avon, Wiltshire
www.ex-librisbooks.co.uk

Printed by Orbit Digital Print, Corsham

ISBN 978-1-906641-37-5

**All enquiries and correspondence
regarding this book should be addressed to the author**

**James Alsop
13 Meridian Walk
Trowbridge
Wiltshire
BA14 9SX**

Front Cover Photo: Saint Mary The Virgin Church, West Kington

Contents

*To Robert Oliver — pastor, preacher,
tutor, mentor and ever faithful friend*

Foreword

In the city of Oxford at the south end of St Giles stands an imposing and ornate memorial, which looks rather like the spire of a sunken cathedral. It was placed there in the nineteenth century to commemorate three men who died just outside the city wall many years before. Two died on the same day, 16 October 1555, when Hugh Latimer and Nicholas Ridley were burned alive. Thomas Cranmer was put to death in the fire on 21 March in the following year. One of those three, Hugh Latimer, is the subject of this book.

Who was Hugh Latimer? What did he do in life, and what was it about him that provoked so strong a response from the religious authorities of his day that they had him put to death in this cruel way? What were his convictions, and what gave him the courage to pay the ultimate price for his faith?

This book has been written to answer these questions and to introduce Hugh Latimer to readers of the twenty-first century, who can discover that this hero of the Christian faith was a witty man who enjoyed life and company, a stimulating and lively preacher and a great champion of the English Bible.

Readers who have enjoyed James Alsop's earlier William Tyndale: An Introduction will already know his warm and approachable style, which draws the reader into sharing his own enthusiasm for his subject.

I am happy to commend this book to all who share Hugh Latimer's faith and to all who may yet discover that faith for themselves.

Ben Elford

Acknowledgements

I would like to thank Ben Elford for his invaluable help and encouragement, without which the book would never have been written! I would also like to thank Dr Robert Oliver for his assistance with some key aspects of historical analysis. Thanks are also extended to Roger Jones for preparing this book for publication. I am indebted to them all.

Introduction

The purpose of this little book is to introduce one of England's most remarkable Christian martyrs, who played a pivotal role in the early reformed period of the sixteenth century. Often referred to as Tyndale's complement (another, more famous, Christian martyr who was the first man to translate the New Testament from the original Greek into everyday English), Latimer's gift was not for languages, but as a popular and practical preacher, who the common people could understand.

Born in the late 1400s at a time when the Church of Rome was 'everywhere in evidence and seemed to be all-powerful'[1], and reared by relatively wealthy parents who were committed Catholics, he was in many respects a most unlikely candidate for conversion to reformed, biblical Christianity, rendering the story of his life all the more striking.

Bright and academically able he spent eighteen years at Cambridge University and established his credentials as one of the nation's most trusted churchmen. However, after a life-changing encounter, when close to forty years of age, with a man by the name of Thomas Bilney (yet another martyr), he underwent a profound religious experience (called conversion) during which he realised that many of the practices of the existing church were corrupt and more superstitious than spiritual. But critically he also came to understand that pardon and forgiveness from God is not obtained through various rituals and practices prescribed by the Church (which often served to enrich it), but through faith in Jesus Christ, as clearly documented in New Testament scripture.

Perilous though the times were for Reformation sympathisers, Latimer lived another thirty years after his conversion, during which he profoundly influenced the nation of England.

Surviving early altercations with angry bishops he became a king's chaplain to Henry VIII, before standing down to become a parish priest in the small village of West Kington in Wiltshire. However, it was during this stage of his life that he faced his biggest crisis. Faced with a choice between compromise or probable death at the stake for heresy, he chose the former, but matured greatly as a result of the experience, and determined to be ready to die for the reformed faith should he be called to account in the same way again.

Both church and state were in a state of flux in the sixteenth century. As a result Latimer was to recover his reputation as a preacher, despite the antagonism that most senior churchmen felt towards him because of his fearless criticism of the Church of Rome. He was even appointed a bishop, in 1535. Although he resigned from this position just four years later, his period in office was one of huge significance; Henry VIII consolidated his break with Rome and his position as head of the Church in England, the dissolution of the largely autonomous monasteries took place, many of the Church's corrupt practices were exposed and the Bible in English received the king's blessing, and was soon after placed in every church in England, with the instruction that it should be read aloud regularly.

After resigning his bishopric, Latimer was placed under house arrest. The next phase of his life was a quiet one, during which his knowledge of the scriptures grew substantially. Then under the short reign of young Edward VI he once again enjoyed influence and the opportunity to preach to a range of audiences. It was during this period more than any other that he earned his reputation as one of the most important preachers in England, as his scholarly skills and common touch enabled him to reach citizens from every walk of life. But when the young king died, England's 'reign of terror' was about to begin.

In 1553 Edward's older sister Mary (known as 'Bloody Mary') became Queen. Not only was she a convinced Catholic, she also wanted to reverse all the progress the reformers had made. Further, she was willing to use extreme (if judicial) violence to do so. Once the burning of reformers commenced in February 1555, the Queen seemed to develop an almost insatiable appetite for this barbaric practice! Hence by November 1558 nearly three hundred Protestant Christians had been executed in this manner. Latimer did not escape this purge, despite (or perhaps because of) his national reputation as a popular preacher of biblical truths, but was summoned to London, to be imprisoned while awaiting a disputation. This took place in Oxford in March 1554, but after being condemned he had a long wait for the inevitable day of execution, which eventually came to pass on the 16 October 1555.

The remarkable account of Latimer's dignity and composure when about to face the agonising flames (recorded in chapter 11) serves as a timeless example of God's sustaining grace to those who are trusting in him and the saving merits of his son, Jesus Christ, and should challenge all readers, whether atheists who are baffled at the failure of Latimer and others to compromise to save themselves from a terrible fate, agnostics genuinely interested in the claims of biblical Christianity or professing Christians who want to be challenged and encouraged in the apathetic times in which we live now. Though Latimer is not as well known as other English or continental reformers, studying his life, conversion, character and role will both challenge and richly reward those who do so with an open mind, not least because his invaluable contribution to the Reformation and Christ-centred biblical Christianity will be clear for all to see.

Finally, this book is deliberately brief, being an introduction to Hugh Latimer and no more, therefore I would urge you to consult the further reading section, where more detailed accounts (by far more gifted authors) of both Latimer and the context of his times can be studied at leisure. Despite the amount of material inevitably left out, I have nevertheless taken special care to ensure that relevant facts have been carefully checked and sources appropriately recorded.

Chapter 1

Life and the Church in Latimer's times

It is not easy for a citizen of modern Britain to imagine just how tough and uncomfortable life was in the late fifteenth and early sixteenth centuries; for though it was (relatively speaking) 'a time of swelling prosperity'[1] for some (e.g. the merchant classes), compared to the lifestyle, comforts and security we enjoy today, life for most was little more than a grim and uncertain slog. In the first instance, infancy itself posed real dangers. Countless young lives were lost due to diseases and illnesses that today have been all but banished from the scene. In raw statistical terms, 25 per cent of all children died before they were five years old and 40 per cent did not reach the age of sixteen.[2] We are told that Latimer himself had several brothers, none of whom survived early childhood. He also had six sisters, but some of these perished during infancy also.[3] Second, only a small minority of children were educated, thus illiteracy was the norm. Latimer was very privileged in this respect, in that he was educated from a young age and spent many years at Cambridge University, one of only two such institutions in England at this point in history. Third, poverty was widespread and often could not be alleviated. Many who were born poor, died poor, and passed on this unhappy lot, from generation to generation. Latimer's position was again a happier one, as his father was a reasonably successful yeoman farmer, who was able to employ half-a-dozen employees.[4] But we should not fall into a complacent mindset of assuming that life on the farm was one of cosseted comfort; on the contrary, the young Latimer would, at times, have experienced hard grind, cold and discomfort, all of which would no doubt have aggravated his already fragile constitution. Fourth, the State, while able to escape from the tyrannical grip of Rome during Latimer's lifetime, provided none of the democratic freedoms we enjoy today (many of which were still centuries away), nor did it provide any safety net for those enduring severe poverty. However, it was not slow to punish the guilty, and those who like Latimer spoke out against corruption within the Church risked being sentenced to death at the stake; a torturous and often excruciatingly painful death that perceived heretics were routinely sentenced to, even long after Henry VIII broke with Rome (in 1533) and became the supreme head of the Church of England. Fifth, disease regularly rampaged through regions of England, leaving many sick and dead in its wake. Treatment was primitive and often based on superstitious practices rather than informed medical knowledge, thus those fortunate enough to survive childhood often faced constant threats to their health and well being. Latimer experienced times of severe weakness and illness, rendering it all the more remarkable that he lived to the age of 70. Sixth, travel was slow, arduous and dangerous, and unsurprisingly therefore, many travelled only short distances, rendering communication difficult.

Having briefly discussed life in those days in general, we now need to consider the role of the Church in Latimer's times. For well over half Latimer's lifetime, England remained under the authority of the Church of Rome, this situation resulting in a number of distinct disadvantages for English citizens.

It was not uncommon for dioceses to be under the authority of absent bishops of foreign nationality who never visited England,[5] but who were happy to accumulate wealth and comfort as a result of their position. Further, the Church itself also accumulated vast sums of money, which increased the impoverishment of ordinary citizens without providing them with any obvious spiritual or material benefit. But of greater importance still were two further critical factors. First, the people of England were denied the Bible in the English language, thus the Church maintained a complete monopoly on Christian teaching, even though such teaching often flatly contradicted biblical doctrine and the teaching of Jesus and the Apostle Paul. And second, corruption, superstition and ignorance were endemic, even among the clergy who should have been showing the common people the way of salvation, and helping to provide for their essential day-to-day needs. In truth, many of the clergy were poor and ignorant themselves, and were only in the Church for the meagre financial rewards they could secure from it. But this resulted in misery and spiritual darkness for parishioners, whose vital needs were being neglected.

From this unlikely context then, the English Reformation was born, and few played a more important role in fostering its steady growth than Hugh Latimer.

Chapter 2

Birth and early life

While it is not possible to be certain, Latimer was probably born in 1485. What is beyond doubt however, is the place of his birth, which was Thurcaston in Leicestershire. His father was a successful yeoman farmer, who at that time were described as 'the real strength of the country, the glory of England, the envy of other nations.'[1] However, this afforded the young Latimer relative comforts and not the levels of wealth and prosperity enjoyed by the few in those days.

Latimer had several brothers who all died in infancy (as previously noted), and six sisters, but little is known of them. His mother probably died when he was a young boy, but again we know very little about her. Latimer himself never married, but used his freedom as a single man to the full, including as a scholar, king's preacher, parish priest, bishop and defender of biblical truths, all of which we shall note as his life's story unfolds.

Despite a weak constitution (which plagued him all his life) Latimer was a bright and lively boy, who when probably no older than four, was described as having 'a ready, prompt and sharp wit'.[2] This tendency stirred his parents to do all they could to supply their young son with an education. It should be noted however, that schools were very rare in Latimer's times, and those that existed were not exactly bursting at the seams with good literature. The printing press was still a recent invention, and therefore printed books were a scarce and precious resource. In all probability Latimer's father would have looked to the Church for educational assistance, first from the parish priest, but also from monks who existed in quite considerable numbers. We should also keep in mind that Latimer's father was a prominent supporter of the Church, and thus he would have been anxious to educate Latimer in the Church's teaching, to ensure he remained a loyal adherent (which for many years he did).

Whatever the quality of young Latimer's education, we know that in 1506 he 'went up' to Cambridge and began studying for his Bachelor of Arts degree. This he successfully achieved in 1510, before continuing to study for a Master of Arts. He achieved his masters in 1514, but between 1510 and 1514 he was also ordained and thus became a priest as well as a student. In 1524, after eighteen years at Cambridge, Latimer achieved his Bachelor of Divinity, completing a long and distinguished university career, all of it within the bosom of the Church, and not as a reformer zealous to change England for good. In fact, Latimer was described at the end of this period as 'one of the great champions of the Church and the old learning in the University', and as one for whom 'there was no great risk of any change taking place in his opinions'.[3] How remarkable then that such a dramatic change was to occur, which in some respects can be likened to the Damascus Road conversion of Saul into the Apostle Paul, especially in terms of the effect it had on the wider Church in England.

Before moving on, there is a vital link we need to establish between Latimer's distinguished university career and his dramatic conversion. As a result of becoming a Bachelor of Divinity Latimer was required to deliver a lecture to the entire university. Keen to be relevant and contemporary, he preached on the importance of resisting the call of the heretics for the Bible in English, emphasising how the Church was the sole authority on Christian doctrine. Listening to the lecture was Thomas Bilney, who had already undergone a Bible-based conversion and who wanted to share his joy and new learning with others. As Bilney listened to Latimer he recognised his preaching skills, but witnessed a man who possessed 'zeal without knowledge'.[4] Bilney was emboldened by the experience and therefore decided to meet Latimer in order to share biblical truths with him, and in the next chapter we shall discover how the meeting developed, after first learning a little more about Bilney the evangelist.

Chapter 3

An unexpected conversion

Thomas Bilney, affectionately called 'Little Bilney'[1] by Latimer, was an able and energetic scholar, but he was also physically weak, fragile, timid, quiet and of small stature. Labouring for years under the weight of a guilty conscience in the sight of a holy God, he was desperate to find peace of mind. Typical of the vast majority of English people in such a situation at this time in history, he repeatedly turned to the Church in search of hope for his soul. However, these attempts were in vain and only worsened his state of mind. The account of what happened next is best described by Bilney himself, as it arguably amounts to one of the most significant and heart warming religious experiences in the life of the reformed Christian Church.

> 'I also, miserable sinner, before I could come unto Christ, had spent all that I had upon ignorant physicians, that is to say, unlearned hearers of confession; so that there was but small force of strength left in me (who of nature was but weak), small store of money, and very little wit or understanding; for they appointed me fastings, watchings, buying of pardons and masses; in all which things (as I now understand), they sought rather their own gain, than the salvation of my sick and languishing soul. But at last I heard speak of Jesus, even then when the New Testament was first set forth by Erasmus (i.e. AD 1516); which when I understood to be eloquently done by him, being allured by the Latin rather than by

the word of God (for at that time I knew not what it meant), I bought it, even by the providence of God – as I do now well understand and perceive – and, at the first reading, as I well remember, I chanced upon this sentence of St. Paul (Oh most sweet and comfortable sentence to my soul!) in 1 Timothy 1: "It is a true saying, and worthy of all men to be embraced, that Christ Jesus came into the world to save sinners, of whom I am the chief and principal." This one sentence, through God's instruction and inward working, which I did not then perceive, did so exhilarate my heart, being before wounded with the guilt of my sins, and being almost in despair, that immediately I felt a comfort and quietness, insomuch that my bruised bones leaped for joy.'[2]

As well as the joy and liberation Bilney knew and felt at this point in his life, two other striking factors are worthy of our attention. First, he systematically described all the rituals the Church had set out for him in order to find peace, but which came at a real financial cost to himself while providing a source of income for the Church. Second, when he began to read the New Testament it was not primarily because he hoped to find the answer to his most urgent need, rather he was impressed by Erasmus's scholarly achievements. Thus the Church had so successfully concealed the truth of scripture that even an able scholar like Bilney, who was desperately seeking peace with, and pardon from God had not appeared to appreciate that the answer to his needs might be contained within scripture itself.

As a changed man, Bilney could not keep the truth to himself, so he began to share his experience and the teaching of scripture (at great personal risk) with others. By the time he attended Latimer's lecture (referred to at the end of the previous chapter), his activities and their growing impact, though largely secretive, were already a cause for concern, hence Latimer's chosen theme for the occasion. But when Bilney decided he must then go and speak with Latimer personally he was entering uncharted waters. Though he had detected a promising zeal in Latimer, he was about to witness to one of the most trusted churchmen in the university, who by definition was hardly an obvious risk-free contact or potential convert.

Bilney's bravery was richly rewarded! Initially, Latimer thought he had come to confess his guilt, but soon realised he was hearing a confession of faith. Despite the fact that Bilney would have told him how reading the scriptures (precisely the act Latimer had just been preaching against) had at last delivered him from the bondage that fastings and vigils had only intensified, Latimer was struck by this 'simple honest soul, who had found the peace that [he] had been seeking in vain.'[3] Latimer's perception was that these heretics, of whom Bilney was the leader, were proud and arrogant men, yet here before him stood (and spoke) one who was gracious, calm and devout. Thus Bilney's witness and words were the means of Latimer's conversion from highly respected churchman to humble, repentant individual, who found peace with God through a personal faith in Jesus Christ, as revealed in the pages of scripture and not through the rituals of the Church.

It was probably in the spring of 1524 that this dramatic change took place in Latimer's life. Bearing in mind that he was very nearly forty years old by this time, it is hardly surprising that he was determined to make up for lost time. Bilney and Latimer became the closest of friends and complemented each other well. One was learned, the other mature and eloquent, and together they would make an invaluable contribution to the Reformation in England. Such was the affection that Latimer had for Bilney, that much later in life he referred to him in these terms:

'The same Bilney was the instrument whereby God called me to knowledge; for I may thank him, next to God, for that knowledge that I have in the word of God. For I was as obstinate a papist as any was in England.'[4]

Owing to his close friendship with Bilney, Latimer joined the early reformers who met at the White Horse tavern in Cambridge, where the New Testament was pored over carefully and discussed at length. These two men were also often to be seen out walking together, on what became known as Heretics Hill. But besides the wonderful friendship they cultivated, Latimer's conversion also resulted in other partnerships, albeit of a much less intimate type. Within two years of the probable date of Latimer's conversion, Tyndale's New Testament (translated from the original Greek for the first time, into a plain and lucid English, and printed in considerable numbers) started to arrive in England via the ports of the south-east. Thus while Tyndale's magnificent work as a linguist brought the scriptures to the ordinary folk of England, Latimer's preaching gifts served as the ideal complement.[5] Though Latimer's conversion occurred around the same time as Tyndale left England to complete his invaluable translation on the Continent,[6] and therefore these two men never conversed face-to-face as fellow believers, their dual significance as vitally important (and complementary) reformers is beyond doubt. Latimer was not a great linguist, however in common with other scholars of his time, he spoke and wrote fluently in Latin as well as English. This enabled him to preach in either language, using the former when preaching to the clergy, and the latter when addressing the common people.[7]

We have now reached a point in the life of Latimer where, liberated and renewed, he was preaching a message of hope based on the scriptures and mixing with fellow reformers, while remaining cautious and, in some respects, orthodox, concerning doctrine, as well as loyal to the Church. But could such an apparent compromise last? How could one who preached from the scriptures avoid the attention of the reformers' enemies? This perplexing question sets the context for much of Latimer's life over the coming years, as the forthcoming chapters will reveal.

Chapter 4

Encountering Wolsey

Bishop West of Ely, suspicious of Latimer and his preaching, was one of the first in authority who tried to put a stop to his exhortations. In 1525, he burst in upon Latimer when he was preaching in an attempt to catch him red-handed. However, Latimer was a skilled and shrewd operator who stopped his sermon, changing the theme in acknowledgement of his additional hearers. Though the contents still infuriated West, he didn't have the incontrovertible evidence for which he had hoped. Not to be defeated in his objective therefore, he asked Latimer to 'preach a sermon against Martin Luther and his doctrine.'[1] This was a skilful (and cunning) move, but Latimer was more than a match for West. Refusing to preach against someone whose works he had never read, he protested his lack of suitability for the task. Incensed by Latimer's reaction, West soon after 'denounced [him] from the pulpit'[2] and removed his licence to preach, in both the diocese and the university. How apparently tragic then, that just as Latimer had begun to preach with directness and clarity as a result of his conversion, that he was to be silenced. But all what not lost, as we shall shortly see.

At first, matters appeared to go from bad to worse for Latimer and any prospects for him preaching again in the foreseeable future. Why was this? A new, outspoken and, at times, rather melodramatic convert, Robert Barnes, had decided to go on the offensive in the most strident terms. On the 24 December 1525,[3] he preached a sermon denouncing the bishops, Cardinal Wolsey in particular. Wolsey was Archbishop of York and papal legate, and had enjoyed a spectacular rise from butcher's son to that of 'the most powerful man in church and state'.[4] However, he was also vain and ambitious, and it was this factor in particular that Barnes had homed in upon.

Barnes's accurate but dramatic and indiscreet sermon provoked a furore, and unsurprisingly therefore, Wolsey decided to investigate him personally. The interrogation to which he was subjected was relentless and eventually he recanted, knowing that if he was ever to speak out in such a way again, he would certainly be burnt at the stake as a relapsed heretic. Barnes's condemnation emboldened the enemies of Latimer and Bilney, and it probably came as no surprise to Latimer that he was subsequently called to answer to Wolsey as well. However, for all Wolsey's vanity he was not an especially cruel man, and he was therefore willing to give Latimer a fair hearing. Satisfied that Barnes had been well and truly disgraced for insulting so senior a churchman as himself, Wolsey was perhaps, almost in a mood of conciliation. Listening to Latimer's denial that he knew anything of Luther's doctrine, he was also struck by Latimer's open and bold conduct. After questioning him further, Wolsey found himself baffled that Latimer had been banned from preaching and sent to him for critical appraisal. Latimer then reported how Bishop West had withdrawn permission for him to preach. Wolsey sympathised with Latimer and appeared to humiliate Bishop West, telling Latimer, 'after a gentle monition'[5] that he could have a licence to preach from Wolsey himself, and that if West didn't like it, Latimer could preach it to his beard! Therefore from such a potentially catastrophic situation, liberty and freedom was to result for one of the early English Reformation's most able preachers.

Latimer returned with haste to Cambridge, and the next time he was in the pulpit he 'read aloud the licence of the Cardinal',[6] much to the delight and relief of his hearers. Further, other reformers summoned to see Wolsey received similarly humane treatment. Thus it appears that the vain Cardinal did, whether intentionally or otherwise, aid the progress of the Reformation in England at a critical juncture.

Chapter 5

Preaching before the king

The king at this point in history of course was Henry VIII, who was a colourful character to say the least. However, despite the myriad reasons for this reputation, including some trivial and some of real significance, he is perhaps best remembered as the king who had six wives. The rhyme that many of us will remember from school history lessons (divorced, beheaded, died, divorced, beheaded, survived) describes the plight of each wife and gives some indication of the king's volatility. But, without doubt, this king more than any other, brought about the seminal changes that enabled the English Reformation to lay down deep and lasting roots, regardless of the motives involved.

Opinion appears divided concerning Henry's qualities as a monarch, but this issue aside, at this stage in our story he was determined to divorce his first wife (Catherine of Aragon), in favour of a much younger and more attractive one (Anne Boleyn). Knowing as we do, how many wives Henry eventually had, it is easy to be entirely cynical about his motives. However, sons born to Catherine were either stillborn or died in infancy. Henry saw it as vital to have a son and heir who could continue the Tudor dynasty. He began therefore to seek expert opinion on whether the marriage to his deceased brother's wife was legitimate according to Church law. Placing Henry in the best possible light, he may have been genuinely concerned about the legitimacy of his marriage, and regarded his son-less state as a judgement from God. Regardless of Henry's true motives, the pope to whom he appealed for an annulment of the marriage deliberately delayed a decision for as long as possible (in reality, indefinitely) so that a difficult decision could be avoided. Henry was furious to be kept waiting for so long, and began to consider a far reaching, alternative option. Were he to break with Rome altogether he could reach a decision and get on with his desired second marriage, and live in hope that a son might be born to him.

Though Henry was a fully committed Catholic in terms of doctrine, he wanted supporters who would appreciate his predicament and favour his suggested break with Rome. Many reformers cautiously backed the argument that his marriage was indeed illegitimate and that therefore, he was free to remarry. Additionally, Anne Boleyn herself was sympathetic to the reformers and would no doubt help their cause if she became Henry's wife. Leaving aside much of the detail, Latimer came to the king's attention, as a preacher of eloquence who was supportive of his concerns over his marriage to Catherine and its probable illegitimacy. Henry decided therefore to hear Latimer for himself. On 13 March 1530[1] Latimer preached to the king and his court, and he was well received. He continued to preach to the king throughout Lent and from this remarkable opening his influence was greatly extended. In recognition of Henry's high regard for Latimer, he was paid £5[2] for his services, a considerable sum for his times.

Despite all the progress that Latimer and the reformers seemed to be making, a setback was to follow. Henry wanted Latimer to join a commission which would investigate the increasing number of religious books in circulation. Those accepted by the commission would be permitted, while those rejected would be banned. Though Latimer was one of the first to be chosen,[3] many of the other commissioners were outright enemies of the Reformation, and therefore he was always likely to be frustrated by the commission's verdicts, as well as by the confusion that his membership of such a commission could cause. Among the condemned books was Tyndale's ground-breaking New Testament, precisely the book English people needed. What could Latimer do in such a situation? Bravely, he took up his pen and wrote to the king personally. In it he asked that the Bible in

English might be available for all to read without censure. Henry responded in a positive, if ambiguous manner, giving Latimer some hope for a brighter tomorrow, though he had to wait until September 1538 for the answer to his request to be implemented.[4] Latimer's letter was not some brief affair, written to assuage a guilty conscience, but was long and detailed. But especially striking was the bold tone of the letter, which Latimer well knew could have cost him his life. Quoted below is just the penultimate paragraph, but this is more than enough to demonstrate Latimer's courage, determination and principled position.

> 'And take heed whose counsels your Grace doth take in this matter, that you may do that God commandeth, and not that seemeth good in your own sight without the Word of God; that your Grace may be found acceptable in his sight, and one of the members of His Church; and, according to the office that He hath called your Grace unto, you may be found a faithful minister of His gifts, and not a defender of His faith: for he will not have it defended by man or man's power, but by His word only, by the which He hath evermore defended it, and that by a way far above man's power or reason, as all the stories of the Bible make mention.'[5]

Despite Latimer's extraordinary boldness, Henry took no action against him and appeared almost to admire his bravery, appointing him as 'a royal chaplain'.[6] However, it was not long before Latimer had had enough of life in such circles, not least because he found that his hearers were much more interested in the latest gossip and trivial arguments than hearing him preach from the scriptures. Helped by friends in high places therefore, he managed to obtain a country parish. Though some were sad to see him depart, he was not for turning, and so on 14 January 1531,[7] he took up his new position as the parish priest of West Kington, a small Wiltshire village, that even to this day boasts no more than a few hundred residents.

Chapter 6

"To West Kington I will go"

It is tempting to assume that Latimer's time at West Kington was one of relative ease after being a royal chaplain, and that he opted for this parish in order to rest from his recent labours. Furthermore, he referred to the parish appointment as his 'little cure',[1] and Demaus, in his authoritative biography states that 'the retirement of West Kington must have brought refreshing and invigorating rest.'[2] However, Latimer was both a hard working and increasingly well known man, for whom a truly quiet life was not a serious option.

Hearers were divided over the merits of the new parish priest, some earnestly welcoming the preaching of a reformer, which no doubt reminded them of the great Bible translator Tyndale, who had worked as a tutor and priest in the nearby Gloucestershire village of Little Sodbury a decade earlier. Others however, especially members of the clergy, were opposed to his biblical teaching and criticism of the Church, and were ready to discredit him whenever possible.

Meanwhile the king had still not obtained the divorce he so desired, but was nevertheless determined to have his way. This state of mind resulted in both positive and negative outcomes for the reformers. But before proceeding to briefly discuss these outcomes we would be wise to note the following. For all the apparent respect Henry had for Latimer, and the promise he had made for the Bible in English at some future point, the king was a complicated and contradictory character, whose volatility added to the erratic nature of the Reformation movement's progress. Yes, he felt insulted by the pope due to the deliberate procrastination over a decision about the proposed divorce, and he clearly admired some of the reformers, however, he was a Catholic at heart, in every sense, who had no real sympathy with reformed doctrine. Separately, at this precise moment in history the Church had not been made fully subservient to Henry's rule, nor had the dissolution of the monasteries taken place, and therefore the Church remained a very powerful institution, dwarfing, and very hostile to, the reformed movement within it.

Moving on to consider the outcomes then, let us first consider them from a positive perspective. The king was coming to the point where he could see no way to make progress unless he could declare himself as head of the English Church in place of the pope. He also simultaneously feared that if he broke with Rome, the reformers would gain too much of a stronghold. So what was he to do? Advised and encouraged by one who was rising in his estimation (Thomas Cromwell), he was persuaded to revive a largely forgotten fourteenth century law that, ironically, forbade any 'appeal to the court of Rome, ---------- or anything that infringed the rights of the Crown.'[3] Needless to say the clergy were shocked, fearful and angry, especially as the implications of the revived law became clear. Despite paying enormous fines to obtain pardon, required retrospectively for their past allegiance to Rome, insult was added to injury when, on 11 February 1531,[4] Henry had to be accepted as 'supreme head of the English Church'.[5] Severely weakening a previously all-powerful Church, this momentous development, though based on questionable motives to say the least, without doubt strengthened the position of the reformers. However, there was also a negative outcome which made life even more difficult for men like Latimer. The clergy were eager for revenge and to prevent any dilution of Catholic dogma, and therefore they were that much more determined to hunt down and ensnare any with heretical tendencies. Perhaps at this point in his life therefore, despite the comforts, quietness and relative solitude of West Kington, Latimer felt as if his enemies were more numerous and vociferous than at any time since his conversion. And in the next chapter we shall see how these enemies homed in on Latimer, as one of their major targets, causing him to waver when facing the most severe challenge of his life so far.

Chapter 7

Dark clouds gather

Latimer's opponents were closing in on him both nationally and locally. Of no little significance, Stokesley, a man vehemently opposed to the Reformed movement, had become Bishop of London. Further, he had made it his intention to try Latimer personally, along with Bilney. Thankfully, Latimer's distance from London placed him beyond Stokesley's grasp, but he had to remain vigilant and cautious nonetheless. But locally he was also very unpopular with a number of the clergy in nearby parishes. In particular, he preached a sermon in the nearby village of Marshfield in which he criticised 'the rulers of the Church in the strongest terms.'[1] Although Stokesley's violence had no doubt angered him in the extreme (together with Sir Thomas More, Stokesley was known to punish heretics using violent means, illegally), his sermon had been misunderstood, exaggerated, and deliberately embellished. But whatever the motives of those spreading rumours about Latimer's sermon may have been, he had nevertheless preached boldly, making his opposition to certain practices and office holders within the Church abundantly clear.

Latimer did in fact venture to London in the summer of 1531, probably in response to a request from friends who wanted to hear him preach again. However, he preached in Kent first, and then in London but only after being repeatedly encouraged to do so. Knowing of Stokesley's personal bitterness towards him, it is no great surprise that Latimer was cautious.

When Latimer was finally persuaded to preach in the capital, word reached Stokesley whose anger was aroused by the reported content, but although he tried to turn the king against Latimer, Henry appeared to take little if any notice of him. Thus the popular preacher returned free and unmolested to West Kington.

At this stage we should once again consider Bilney, and sadly, the final phase of his life. Having previously recanted, as many of the reformers did at this point in time, he had been severely depressed, believing that he had denied his Lord and Saviour Jesus Christ. Gradually though, his strength and courage revived and now he was determined, 'whatever the risk might be, to preach openly those doctrines which he had twice denied.'[2] In his own words he had decided that 'I must needs go up to Jerusalem.'[3] This poignant statement must have produced an emotional response in those who loved him dearly, for now it was obvious that he was determined to pay for such preaching with his life!

Bilney preached first in Norfolk, the county of his birth, and then moved south, distributing Tyndale's New Testament everywhere he went. But when he moved north again, he was finally apprehended. It was the Bishop of Norwich who caught him, after which the sealing of his fate was just a formality. He was sentenced to be burnt on 19 August 1531. Because of the wind direction and strength, for a time the fire burned 'away from his body',[4] thus he suffered agonies as the flames scorched him but did not initially take hold. However, he finally succumbed, thus proving to be a faithful witness to the truth of scripture, even when experiencing almost unimaginable pain (not to mention cruel injustice).

Latimer was deeply distressed when he heard of his invaluable friend's death. No doubt his thoughts returned to the time in his life when Bilney had patiently and boldly explained the way of salvation to him. He would have remembered their long walks and talks on Heretics Hill in Cambridge, and the inspirational discussions in the White Horse tavern. But now his dear friend, one closer than a brother, was dead. And what was to say he would not be the next to suffer such a cruel end?

Stokesley, More and others were not content with the death of Bilney only. On the contrary, his death appeared to whet their appetite, and even, perversely, to assuage their guilty feelings about giving up their authority to Henry so easily.[5] Stokesley, and More in particular, became almost fanatical heretic hunters, operating outside the law, despite the fact that More's considerable credentials as a lawyer left him with no excuse for such behaviour. He even began to torture heretics personally, displaying a barbarity that left any true Christian profession in tatters. Even if More and Stokesley believed themselves to be besieged by the growing reformed movement, Jesus' own words in Matthew 5: 43–45 starkly exposed them:

> "You have heard that it was said, 'Love your neighbour and hate your enemy.' But I tell you: Love your enemies and pray for those who persecute you, that you may be sons of your Father in heaven."

Although Latimer was back in his little parish, far from London (especially by the standards and methods of sixteenth century travel), Stokesley was determined to apprehend him as soon as possible, and to bring him before the bishops and clergy (Convocation) for interrogation. What was Latimer to do? Should he flee to the Continent as others had done, and as some were advising him to do, or should he continue in his parish despite the increasing danger to his life?

Though downcast and anxious, he remained in West Kington, growing in his knowledge of the scriptures, and preaching with as much, if not more earnestness than previously. However, early in January 1532, almost a year to the day from when he had first arrived in the Wiltshire village, a messenger appeared, telling him that he must appear before Stokesley on 29 January.[6]

Latimer was full of apprehension as he undertook the long, cold and tiring journey to London. Shortly he was to face the cruel Stokesley, who had been determined to ensnare him for some time, and whose appetite for displaying cruelty to reformers seemed to intensify not diminish as the number of those tortured and punished increased. Soon his life and liberty would hang by a slender thread, and yet now was the moment when he was going to have to make a stand against the corruptions of the Church, whatever the risk to himself. Further, as already noted, Latimer was not a physically strong man, and at this time in his life he had been suffering from quite severe ill-health, causing him to say (just a few weeks later) that 'My head is out of frame, and my whole body so weak.'[7] Considering the human frailties and fears that men and women of all ages are subject to, especially when facing a life threatening situation, and that his journey would, no doubt, have been a lonely one, we can surely sympathise with him as he neared the capital, praying that he would be kept from denying his Saviour.

On arrival in London, Latimer was not granted a period of rest and relaxation, nor any time to prepare for his ordeal. Stokesley and several other bishops began the trial without delay. The practical challenges of such a situation must have been trying enough, but what were Latimer's thoughts as he pondered the fact that the truths and experiences so precious to him (including the momentous occasion when Bilney entered his study and graphically described his conversion) were anathema to Stokesley, and were likely to engender more hatred and anger in the man and his associates? We should also remember that Latimer was still relatively new to the reformed faith and had to contend with possible confusion in his own mind, as he tried to reconcile scriptural truths with what he still believed to be the best of the Church's teaching.

As the trial proceeded, Latimer had another challenge to overcome. Initially, the room in which he was being tried had been warmed by a fire burning in the grate. But as the days passed the fire was no more, and instead a cloth hung over the fireplace.[8] Furthermore, as Latimer answered the questions posed, one of his accusers asked him to speak up. Then, as he listened carefully, the reason for this mysterious change became clear. Behind the cloth, at the base of the chimney, someone was recording his every word, in the hope of producing some vital piece of evidence against him. Had fear, anger and sadness been his dominant emotions at this moment, who could honestly have blamed him? But Latimer described how he was trusting solely in God, and as a result was able to resist their subsequent questions, which had been carefully crafted to trap him. In his own words he said of the occasion:

> 'But God, which always hath given me answer, helped me, or else I could never have escaped it; and delivered me from their hands.'[9]

The trial lasted for six weeks after which Latimer was handed over to Convocation. Eventually on 11 March 1532,[10] Latimer was ordered to either admit to being a heretic or accept the very abuses he had consistently spoken out against. On three occasions he resolutely refused to sign up to a series of articles which, taken as a whole, amply display the anti-scriptural teaching of which the Church of Rome was guilty at this point in history. While these articles are quite numerous and extend an already lengthy chapter for a book of this size, this issue is of such significance that they are recorded below, with some being followed by a few brief comments, in italics, which are intended to indicate the stark difference between the doctrine of Rome and that of the scriptures, which Latimer had come to cherish.

The Articles

1/ I believe that there is a purgatory to purge the souls of the dead.

2/ That the souls in purgatory are holpen (helped) by the masses, prayers and alms of the living.

(The following comments and scriptural quotations are relevant to

articles 1 and 2.)

Nowhere in the New Testament, whether it be the teachings of Jesus, the Apostle Paul, any other apostle or any other author of a New Testament book, will you find any reference to the intermediate state of purgatory! On the contrary, the entire thrust of New Testament theology is based on the need to be ready for judgement at the point of death. The writer to the Hebrews emphasises this point when he says:

> *'Just as a man is destined to die once, and after that to face judgement, so Christ was sacrificed once to take away the sin of many people;' (Hebrews 9:27–28)*

But ponder also the words of the Apostle Paul who states in his first letter to the Corinthians:

> *'I tell you, now is the time of God's favour, now is the day of salvation.' (I Corinthians 6:2)*

Yet perhaps surpassing both of the above references are the words of Jesus to the dying thief, who was crucified beside him. In a spirit of true repentance, which has served for the past two thousand years as a reminder of God's saving grace to the genuinely penitent, the thief turned to Jesus, after rebuking the other criminal crucified at the time, and said:

> *'Jesus, remember me when you come into your kingdom.' (Luke 23:42)*

To which Jesus replied:

> *'I tell you the truth, today you will be with me in paradise.' (Luke 23:43)*

If there was a purgatory surely this thief could not have escaped it.

Still further, when read on a stand alone basis, article two is especially revealing of the Church's error and cynicism. Why is this so? Because if the souls of the dead could be helped by the gifts of the living, then the Church could maintain an almost inexhaustible source of income, regardless of the morality or doctrinal authenticity of such a position.

3/ That the saints in heaven pray for us as mediators.

4/ That the saints should be honoured.

5/ That the invocation of saints is profitable.

6/ That pilgrimages and oblations to the relics and sepulchres of saints are meritorious.

There is not a shred of scriptural evidence, either by direct commendation or inference of any kind, that pilgrimages to the relics and sepulchres of saints (dead saints of course – this point requiring emphasis because New Testament scripture often refers to living Christians as saints) are meritorious. On the contrary, in his letter to the Ephesian Church, the Apostle Paul states in crystal clear terms that:

'For it is by grace you have been saved, through faith—and this not from yourselves, it is the gift of God—not by works, so that no one can boast.' (Ephesians 2:8–9)

Pilgrimages and oblations bring bondage, while God's love in Jesus Christ brings peace and pardon, leading to good works as evidence of repentance, not as works of merit in their own right.

7/ That persons under a vow of perpetual chastity may not marry without a personal dispensation from the Pope.

8/ That the keys of binding and loosing committed to St. Peter remain with his successors the Bishops of Rome, even though they live wickedly; and were not given to laymen.

This is the most extraordinary article of all, leaving the sixteenth century Church of Rome starkly exposed. But the Apostle Peter is best placed to condemn such an erroneous statement, and in his first of two New Testament letters he writes:

'Therefore, prepare your minds for action; be self-controlled; set your hope fully on the grace to be given you when Jesus

> *Christ is revealed. As obedient children, do not conform to the evil desires you had when you lived in ignorance. But just as he who called you is holy, so be holy in all you do; for it is written: "Be holy, because I am holy." ' (1Peter 1:13–16)*

9/ That fasting, prayer, and other good works merit favour at God's hands.

> *Though appearing rather more innocuous than some of the articles, this too has an erroneous element at its core. Jesus exposes it in the parable of the Pharisee and the Tax Collector, recorded in Luke's gospel. Though a more substantial quotation than those above, it is recorded in full to illustrate the extent to which the Church was out of step with scripture generally and the teaching of Jesus in particular.*

> *"Two men went up to the temple to pray, one a Pharisee and the other a tax collector. The Pharisee stood up and prayed about himself: 'God, I thank you that I am not like other men — robbers, evildoers, adulterers — or even like this tax collector. I fast twice a week and give a tenth of all I get.' "But the tax collector stood at a distance. He would not even look up to heaven, but beat his breast and said, 'God, have mercy on me a sinner.' " I tell you that this man, rather than the other, went home justified before God. For everyone who exalts himself will be humbled, and he who humbles himself will be exalted."* (Luke 18:10–14)

10/ That persons forbidden by the Bishop to preach, should not preach until they have purged themselves before him.

11/ That Lent and other fasts should be observed.

12/ That in every one of the seven sacraments grace is obtained by those who rightly receive.

13/ That consecrations and benedictions are laudable and profitable.

14/ That the crucifix, and other images of saints should be kept in churches as memorials, and to the honour and worship of

Jesus Christ and his saints.[11]

Though much more could be said about these articles, the quotations provided help to explain why Latimer robustly rejected them as a whole and, as mentioned above, was prepared to do so three times. However, what happened next, including especially, Latimer's own actions, was to be of sad significance. On the 21 March,[12] he was again summoned by the bishops who appeared to offer a compromise. They informed Latimer that if he could sign up just to articles 11 and 14, they would release him. Latimer considered this a fair compromise and agreed to sign. However, this act did not bring the instantaneous freedom he had hoped for, neither was he able to return swiftly to his relatively quiet country parish. Stokesley demanded that he apologise on his knees (a humiliating ritual indeed) and Convocation insisted that he read to them a confession.[13] Even then Latimer's ordeal was not over. He was detained for another three weeks, and then appeared once more before Convocation, who no doubt hoped to obtain further concessions from him. In fact there is some confusion as to whether or not Latimer relented further and signed the rest of the articles, historical records being unreliable on this point. But this has to be unlikely when following developments logically and objectively. Still Latimer was not a free man, and thus with no other option open to him perhaps, he appealed to the king as supreme head of the Church of England. This was a shrewd move, but one that was not without serious consequences for Latimer's testimony to the truth of scripture and his support for the infant reformed movement. Why was this? Quite simply because Henry supported his appeal, but only on the basis that Latimer would 'make a full and explicit apology'.[14]

Appearing before Convocation once again on 22 April,[15] Latimer had to confess how he had erred from the true teaching of the Church, but after apologising one more time he was finally pardoned by Stokesley. However, it was still another three months before he was a free man able to resume his responsibilities as a parish priest.

How are we to reflect on this sad chapter of Latimer's life? Many reformers (along with others who shared no sympathy with the reformed movement) were quick to judge Latimer, and to condemn the compromises that he made. Even the balanced, analytical and generously spirited Demaus (arguably Latimer's finest and most thorough biographer) appears to join the voices of condemnation as the following quotation reveals:

'This is the darkest page in Latimer's history, and no attempt has been made in any way to conceal or extenuate his weakness. Something might no doubt be urged in his defence: he was constitutionally weak; he was over-persuaded by his friends; he was overawed by Henry; he had not been guilty of apostasy, for he still honestly adhered to almost all the doctrines of the Romish Church. But making all possible allowance for these considerations, it cannot be denied that Latimer's conduct on his trial was unworthy of his character and his position. Caution and prudence in preserving life are admirable virtues; but there are emergencies when it becomes all true men to face danger, and to recognise that there are causes more sacred even than life. His timidity could not but have a disastrous effect wherever his influence extended; the friends of the reformation would be perplexed and alarmed at this weakness in one who seemed their bravest leader; its enemies would be more than ever convinced that, by the proper threats of severity, heresy might be effectually crushed.'[16]

However, perhaps now is the time to offer a few words in defence of Latimer, who at this moment faced severe pressures. What follows therefore is a brief series of (numbered) reasons why his actions and the consequent predicament in which he found himself were understandable at least.

1/ As previously noted, he was a weak man who had been suffering from especially ill health of late. This is an easily overlooked factor, especially when we consider the difficult decisions he was trying to make; who of us, when experiencing physical frailty through poor health, has not perceived the burdens of life intensifying, and with it the impairment of our judgement?

2/ It is probable that well-meaning friends helped to persuade Latimer to compromise (as alluded to in the above quotation). Further, these friends were either fully supportive of, or at least sympathetic to the Reformation. Ignoring the advice of a friend given in ignorance is one thing, remaining immovable when advised by those who understand the issues at stake is quite another.

3/ Although Henry was happy to accept Latimer's somewhat desperate appeal, he did so only with a substantial condition— that he apologise to the bishops! Latimer might well have argued to himself that to ignore the king's condition when in real need of his support could spell disaster, whereas on the other hand, were he to heed the advice, not only would he escape but he might also return fully to the king's favour at some point in the future.

4/ For forty years Latimer's thinking had been entirely in line with the Church's doctrine, and even now he still accepted much of the Church's teaching, hence he could argue that signing up to just two minor articles was hardly a major compromise.

5/ Perhaps as Latimer spent long periods alone, waiting with some uncertainty to know the outcome of his trial, his own father's instruction may have returned to his mind, increasing still further the confusion and anxiety he was experiencing. While there is no evidence for this, it is surely conceivable that in his exhausted state, such emotive thoughts entered his head.

6/ Latimer was a lonely man during the trial period, and he may have felt as though he was arguing against the entire Church of Rome, with all its traditions, authority and power. Were this so, one can easily imagine him asking the question, can I alone be right while all the Church is wrong?

7/ It is clear from the narrative of events that Latimer was slowly drawn, step by step, into progressively greater compromise, and therefore had he known how matters would develop, he might have been more careful before agreeing to sign articles 11 and 14.

8/ We know Latimer did not believe in dying unnecessarily, and perhaps this increased his caution and willingness to give ground.

9/ Real and intense fear could well have overcome Latimer as he thought of the potential outcome of failing to submit to the bishops. Those sentenced to death in such a context as this, invariably died at the stake, an intensely cruel and barbaric punishment that even the bravest of men and women could be intimidated at the thought of. Death was rarely swift as the flames took time to reach vital organs; sometimes limbs fell away while the condemned remained in agony waiting for the inevitable but painfully slow end. Could you or I face such a punishment without especial grace?

10/ The Bible contains many accounts of great men who failed when filled with fear, including Abraham, Moses, Elijah, Peter and others. Though this amounted to desperate failure on their part, they were all restored and forgiven, as the scriptural records make clear. Latimer's weakness however, was arguably more ambiguous and while he learnt much from it, he did not engage in a full denial of the truths to which he had committed himself since his radical conversion.

This list is by no means a complete analysis of the reasons for Latimer's compromise and apparent timidity, but I hope it goes some way to making us think more holistically about the pressures he faced at this perilous moment for both the reformed movement and himself.

Prior to Latimer's eventual release and return to West Kington, he had an encounter with a condemned heretic which had a profound impact on him. Therefore, before bringing this chapter to a close, a brief outline of the occasion is provided. James Bainham, a lawyer 'well known for his charity and piety',[17] was due to be burnt at the stake the day following his brief meeting with Latimer. Having been tortured and interrogated by More he at first recanted, but filled with guilt and a sense of shame, he subsequently declared in a local church that he had denied his Lord and Saviour, and boldly warned others not to give way to fear and intimidation as he had done. Needless to say, this open confession of faith resulted in his swift arrest and condemnation.

Talking with him in Newgate prison, Latimer became convinced that Bainham had decided to give up his life, which alarmed him due to his concerns about sacrificing human life too readily. He even appeared to admonish Bainham saying 'yet beware of vain-glory; for the devil will be ready now to infect you therewith, when you shall come into the multitude of the people.'[18] In a true spirit of graciousness Bainham thanked Latimer for his words of encouragement and advice. However, noticing Latimer's own weakness, he offered the following words of exhortation in return: 'I likewise do exhort you to stand to the defence of the truth; for you that shall be left behind had need of comfort.'[19]

Thus with Bainham's gentle charge ringing in his ears, Latimer bade him farewell, knowing that the very next day, 30 April, he would suffer the same fate as Bilney and one that he had himself only just escaped. Soon after, he left London to return to his country parish, shaken, chastened and even a little confused perhaps, but determined to know the scriptures better, and to learn from the mistakes he had made when capitulating to the will of the bishops.

The carved wooden pulpit from which Latimer preached when parish priest of West Kington (still in use today)

The interior of Saint Mary The Virgin Church, West Kington, where Latimer preached between 1531 and 1535

Stained glass window in Saint Mary The Virgin Church, with the inscription: Hugh Latimer. Bishop and martyr. Some time rector of this parish

A plaque to mark the location (in Oxford) where Latimer was put to death and where he uttered those timeless words: 'Be of good comfort Master Ridley, and play the man. We shall this day light such a candle, by God's grace, in England, as I trust shall never be put out.'

Chapter 8

Latimer the bishop

Not long after Latimer had returned to the relative safety of West Kington, Convocation and the powers of the bishops were rendered invalid.[1] This was a development that aided the reformers as it marked a further, major decline in the power of the Church that was so intent on persecuting them. This meant that the king's permission would always be needed before Convocation could act. To the once mighty Sir Thomas Moore, for whom the Church of Rome would always be the highest authority under God, this was simply too much to swallow. More resigned therefore on the 16 May 1532.[2] What a volatile world sixteenth century England must have been. Just a few weeks earlier Latimer's life had hung by a thread as Stokesley, More and the bishops in general had forced him into a humiliating retreat. But now the scene was set for real and lasting progress to be made by the reformers!

The king had still not secured his divorce at this stage, and now that he had declared himself to be the head of the Church there was, in reality, no prospect of the pope granting his request. Thus he turned to Convocation, seeing an opportunity to have his first marriage annulled at last. The then Archbishop of Canterbury (Warham) died in August of 1532, and this provided the King with a vital opportunity. If he could identify a suitable candidate for the vacant post, he could finally obtain the divorce and marry Anne Boleyn. Henry decided to choose Thomas Cranmer. This decision alone was of enormous significance for the Reformation in England. Cranmer, though not without his flaws and key weaknesses, was a reformer through and through. His knowledge of scripture was substantial and he had begun to comprehend the biblical doctrine of justification by faith alone, rather than relying on the superstitious practices and dictates of the Church. Though he would have to be cautious and careful at all times, to ensure Henry's volatile temperament was not aroused, he would also be able to secure real progress for the Reformation movement.[3]

Henry was shrewd enough to realise that Cranmer needed to be consecrated by the pope, thus he kept a low profile concerning the divorce and his marriage to Anne while waiting for the pope's blessing on Cranmer's appointment. However, once Cranmer was consecrated the six year divorce question could be resolved. Under Cranmer's guidance the divorce was officially granted and the King's marriage to Anne was publicly acknowledged.

This period must have felt like a temporarily new era for Latimer and the reformers. The bishops' powers had been severely curtailed while Henry was indebted, in part, to Cranmer who had helped him finally secure the much coveted divorce. But yet more positive developments were to follow. Cranmer bravely asked the king if Latimer could, once again, preach before 'the court in Lent'.[4] This request was granted and Latimer was permitted to preach weekly between February and March 1534.[5] What a contrast Latimer's journey to London must have been with that of two years previously! Gone was the immediate risk to life and liberty and in its place was royal favour once more.

As Parliament grew bolder, yet more good news followed for the reformers. Despite Henry's commitment to Catholic dogma, more and more authority was being stripped from the Church of Rome as English law was released from its clutches after centuries of subservience. There was an extraordinary irony at the heart of this process, the essence of which was that while 'the legislation of Parliament was as prompt and decisive as the boldest reformer could have wished',[6] Parliament itself strove to make clear that such legislation did not stem from anti-catholic motives, but from a desire to be free from foreign influence and domination.

These momentous events, though not amounting to an unambiguous embrace of Reformation doctrine, were nothing less than a revolution, without which the full future Reformation could not have been secured. To emphasise the high drama of these times still further, More, who was unable to accept Henry as head of the Church in England was eventually sentenced to death, and thus this literary and legal genius turned cruel persecutor of Bible-believing Christians, was executed in early July 1535. Unlike the heretics he was spared the flames, being beheaded—a relatively humane form of execution by comparison with the torture of the stake.

The new Queen Anne, being very sympathetic to the reformers, loved Latimer's preaching and was always keen to hear him. But the King enjoyed his preaching too. Yet for all the exciting progress, it still remained a volatile time for the fledgling Reformation movement, as the King had still not granted the Bible in English to go forth with his blessing, reformed clergy remained in a tiny minority (even though Cranmer, the Archbishop, was a Bible devotee) and preachers like Latimer were scarce to say the least. But even this apparently bleak situation brought further benefits at a critical time. How could this be so? In 1534, Parliament had pronounced that the bishoprics of Worcester and Salisbury were vacant, as they had been previously held by absent Italian bishops. Cranmer and Cromwell (the king's chief minister) were both very keen to secure one of these vacant posts for Latimer, and as he had been supportive of the king, it came as no surprise that he, though not in the least bit ambitious, was appointed to the bishopric of Worcester on 12 August 1535.[7]

Although Latimer remained a bishop for less than four years (from September 1535 to July 1539 to be precise) they were nevertheless some of 'the most momentous years in the history of the English Church and nation.'[8] Summarising briefly, some of the key reasons for this assertion are as follows.

While Latimer was Bishop of Worcester Anne Boleyn was tried and executed, the dissolution of the monasteries took place (changing England dramatically and for ever), the Bible in English was finally authorised by the King, and soon after placed in every church in the country, and a reformed Church, backed by documented articles, began to emerge.

Latimer's diocese was very substantial, stretching a long way south of what we know today as the Midlands, and incorporating the Gloucester and Bristol localities. Further, he was conscious that for long periods his diocese had been under the authority of absentee bishops, and that the spiritual needs of the inhabitants had been neglected. Therefore he was determined to work hard to right long-term wrongs and to promote a return to scriptural principles as opposed to superstitious traditions.

While Latimer busied himself amongst his parishioners and with myriad other pressing responsibilities, the king was already cooling in his affection for Anne! Another woman, Jane Seymour, had attracted his attention and interest, and now he was looking for reasons to be rid of his second wife. Tragically, those opposed to the growing Reformation hated Anne, believing that she had been far too sympathetic to the movement. Could anything be done to prevent Anne's demise and the inevitable threat this would pose to her life in volatile, sixteenth century England? Though Latimer was not physically at hand (being occupied in his diocese) he was the one person who might be able to issue a rebuke to the king. Aware of this fact he seized his opportunity. It was very much the tradition for bishops to present the king with a New Year gift, thus Latimer realised that this was the point at which to act. While other (often much richer) bishops gave Henry very large sums of money, Latimer presented him with a copy of Tyndale's New Testament—the very Bible translation he hated—and a napkin that bore the inscription 'fornicators and adulterers God will judge'![19] Though Henry was no doubt furious to receive such a gift (and stinging rebuke) he did not react or seek to punish

Latimer for it. Sadly however, neither did he alter his behaviour towards either the Queen or Jane Seymour.

Anne was beheaded on the dubious and probably cynical charge of immoral conduct, on 19 May 1536,[10] the king's sordid delight being thinly disguised at best, and his guilt compounded by the fact that the very next day he was betrothed to marry Jane Seymour. No sober reflections then for Henry, not even in the form of pseudo sadness. What's more, within two weeks they were married, unless of course one counts betrothal as marriage, in which case the deed had been completed within just twenty four hours of Anne's cruel execution. While Latimer had no more than an arm's length interest in the sad process, his silence at the time, and subsequently, leaves him wanting at this point. Anne had been a faithful friend of the reformers, and the accusations against her had more than a whiff of foul play about them, thus a principled and typically brave man like Latimer should have been emboldened to chastise the king mildly at least. In fact, bearing in mind his growing maturity as a Bible-believing Christian, one might argue that his faults were more striking, if less dramatic, at this point than when he capitulated before Convocation (see chapter 7).

Meanwhile, more positive developments were occurring elsewhere. In the autumn of 1535 a new translation of the Bible in English had been completed and released on the Continent. Soon after, it reached England. This was Miles Coverdale's version. Though the king gave no more than oral approval to it (doing nothing to aid its distribution therefore), it was yet another important step forward. Combined with the continuing circulation of Tyndale's ground-breaking New Testament, England was slowly changing from a nation which knew nothing of the scriptures, to one which owned, read and prized them.

Separately, despite Henry's preoccupation with the various women in his life, he was determined to attempt to reconcile the various factions within Convocation. As a result, the bishops were called together to agree and sign up to Ten Articles. I have not recorded them here, but suffice to say although they represented a compromise between the beliefs of Rome's adherents and those of the reformers, they were nevertheless an improvement and one more step in the nation's journey towards embracing a protestant theology.

However, as we reflect on events with the benefit of hindsight, overshadowing this entire period was the death of one of England's greatest sons. In October 1536 (probably the 6th),[11] William Tyndale was strangled and then burnt at the stake, after being incarcerated for sixteen months in a grim prison just outside Brussels. This linguistic genius and gracious Christian man was to set England (and the English language) ablaze with his visionary work, even though he died in a state of uncertainty concerning what his work had and would go on to achieve. Latimer was distraught on hearing of his death, no doubt mourning the loss of one to whom England owed so much, and fearing the implications for the reformed movement. But despite the tragic circumstances leading to his execution, and the understandable sense of foreboding that hung over many reformers in England in the immediate aftermath of his passing, many of his ambitious objectives had been achieved including his original 1526 New Testament translation, a 1534 New Testament revision and the translation of several Old Testament books, and had already begun to bring about an inexorable change in the very soul of the nation of England. In addition, though Tyndale the fugitive was never able to return to his native country to witness the growing impact of his work, his influence is still today everywhere apparent, in both the general language of the English speaking people of the world, and the reading and studying of the Bible in English, in churches, colleges, private homes and in any number of more informal environments.

There were also some other key events in this period that should not escape our attention. On the 12 October 1537, a son 'was at last born to Henry'.[12] While this event may not seem of especial significance to the average citizen of twenty first century Britain, its importance at the time can hardly be overstated. The king had been on the throne for twenty eight years and his health was already on the wane.[13] Until this point there had been no heir, and his two daughters—Elizabeth and Mary—were not considered legitimate, thus had either attempted to take the throne at such a time as this, it may well have led to civil war.[14] Further, the king, despite all his faults and failings, had aided the progress of the Reformation greatly, and without an heir the ensuing instability would probably have contributed to a more substantial and permanent reversal of all the reformers had achieved. However, for Henry great sadness followed this happy and momentous event; the Queen died just twelve days after Prince Edward's birth.[15]

The following year (1538), was probably the busiest for Latimer during his short time as a bishop. But more importantly it was also the year of greatest progress for the reformers during Henry's long reign. Being of necessity selective, let us consider just two of the key developments which helped to consolidate the Reformation. First, Latimer had long spoken out and preached against relics and images (of Mary and other saints), but now Archbishop Cranmer was determined that these should be revealed for what they were—terrible frauds, which raked in money for the Church, but did nothing to benefit the souls of pilgrims. Many images that supposedly contained miraculous powers, were brought out into public places, and shown to be the work of deceivers. Such exposure greatly pleased Latimer, as the superstitious spell which bound so many in England was fatally weakened. Second, in September the king finally decided that the Bible in English would be made available to all the people of England. It is scarcely possible to exaggerate the positive changes this one decree brought about in England. Not only did it transform the religious landscape of the country as centuries of superstitious practice were swept away and replaced by rational scriptural teaching, but it also led to substantial secular benefits. Why was this so? Because it helped to consolidate the English language, which until this time had been no more than a North European irrelevance, and became the instrument through which numerous citizens learned to read and to educate themselves. The king also decreed that an English Bible should be placed (and read regularly) in every church in England, an objective that was largely achieved by the following April. Why a monarch of such mixed motives and clear Catholic sympathies should have acted in such a way will always remain something of a mystery, but for the reformers it was the clearest evidence that God was blessing his Church and leading it out from centuries of darkness into the glorious light and liberty of New Testament theology; a theology of justification by faith alone and not through works, beautifully summed up in the words of Jesus, when he said to the religious leader Nicodemus, who came to him by night:

'For God so loved the world that he gave his one and only son, that whoever believes in him should not perish but have eternal life.' (John 3:16)

However 1539 brought a rather dramatic halt to the exciting progress of previous years (and in particular 1538). The king, determined to bring unity to a divided church, instructed a special committee to establish some new articles in the hope that divisions could be overcome and ended for good. But as had happened in the past, the committee consisted of men with diametrically opposed views. Further, those with Reformation sympathies were clearly in the minority, therefore Latimer and Cranmer were never likely to be happy with the outcome of their deliberations.

Six articles were proposed and introduced to the House of Lords, but the man responsible for informing the Lords was happy to pronounce that he had never read the scriptures and had absolutely no intention of doing so! Apart from the obvious implications such a statement had for the nature of the articles, it is worth pausing for just a moment to consider the irony of such a proclamation. Here we have a committee of so-called specialists drawing up articles intended to unify the Church, but one of its most prominent commissioners is pleased to boast his complete ignorance of the scriptures! Perhaps by way of an imperfect example we could liken it to a supposed expert on Shakespeare, who had been invited to chair a committee charged with analysing his works, proudly announcing that he had never read a single one of his plays, nor was he ever going to!

Predictably the articles were completely unsatisfactory and 'put England back years'.[16] Latimer was distraught and became vexed as to what he should do. But what he did next and his reasons for doing so have an element of mystery about them. Latimer resigned his bishopric on 1 July just three days after the articles passed into law. However, it is uncertain whether he resigned regardless of the king's wishes or because he had been informed (inaccurately) that Henry wanted him to do so. Whichever it was, Latimer left office with a sense of relief. Why was this when the articles had so saddened him? Because the manifold responsibilities of his bishopric were now removed. But we should not assume that Latimer was free to return to his favourite vocation—that of preaching to the common people of England. The king was far from happy with Latimer, considering his resignation as 'a censure of his policy by one whom he highly esteemed',[17] and therefore the former bishop was placed under house arrest. This predicament limited Latimer's freedom of movement but not his liberty to entertain friends, thus the consequences of his resignation, though serious, were not dire.

'For the eight years that followed his resignation, the history of Latimer's life is almost a blank.'[18] And so with this important fact in mind we will now move on from 1539 to 1547, when Henry's reign finally came to an end after thirty seven years, the king being fifty six years of age. At this point Latimer was in prison in the dreaded Tower of London (typically referred to as just the Tower) having been sent there in May 1546, after appearing before the Privy Council under further charges of heresy. We should also note that during the period we have passed over the king married three more times, in January 1540 (to Anne of Cleeves), then in August of the same year (to Catherine Howard), and finally in July 1543 (to Catherine Parr—a young woman of about thirty). In the next chapter, we will briefly discover how once again the Reformation progressed, prior to the tumultuous years of 'Bloody Mary'.

Chapter 9

A new king reigns

Edward VI was only nine years old when he became king. However, he was wholeheartedly in favour of the Reformation, and therefore, combined with a general pardon which resulted in Latimer's release from the Tower, the prospects for the progress of the English Reformation were promising indeed. Many wanted to see Latimer restored to the office of bishop, but he would have none of it. Rather, he saw himself as a preacher and evangelist who had a message for all the people of England. Here again we are reminded of how appropriate it was for Latimer to be called Tyndale's complement. Though the latter had now been dead more than ten years, Latimer was continuing and extending Tyndale's work. While Tyndale had produced an English version of the Bible that all the people of England could understand and relate to, regardless of whether they could read or not, Latimer was now preaching and applying that same word of God to eager hearers.

Latimer was now becoming the 'greatest preacher of his day',[1] helped more than a little by the eight years of relative silence (1539–1547), during which he had diligently searched the scriptures and grown in his knowledge and understanding of them. Sadly it is not possible to explore in detail Latimer's preaching style, structure and content, but just in passing we will focus for a moment on one of his most famous sermons. In the 'Sermon of the Plough', Latimer likens preaching to the labour of a ploughman. Much has to be done to prepare listeners for the message of the gospel, but then hearers are expected to respond and turn in repentance to God, just as a ploughman expects to see positive results after all his hard preparatory labour. But then in a fascinating development Latimer proceeds to ask a vital question:

'There is one that passeth all the other, and is the most diligent prelate in all England. And will ye know who it is? I will tell you: it is the devil. He is the most diligent of all other: he is never out of his diocese;---------- Where the devil is resident and hath his plough going, there away with books and up with candles; away with Bibles and up with beads; away with the light of the Gospel, and up with the light of the candles, yea, at noon-days. Where the devil is resident that he may prevail, up with all superstition and idolatry, censing, painting of images, candles, palms, ashes, holy water, and new service of men's inventing, as though man could invent a better way to honour God than God himself hath appointed:'[2]

The above brief quotation alone gives a very clear indication of the refreshing directness and urgency with which Latimer challenged his hearers.

One of the most significant developments for the reformed movement occurred (probably) in September 1548. This was the rejection by both Latimer and Cranmer of the doctrine of transubstantiation, which is the belief that during Catholic Mass, the bread and wine literally become the body and blood of Christ. This issue was central to the doctrinal debate between the Church of Rome and the reformed movement. Why was this? Because if Christ died and was a sacrifice for sin once for all,[3] then the communion service was a memorial but also a spiritual one with Christ, as Christ himself made clear when he said, 'do this in remembrance of me' (1 Corinthians 11:24).[4] But if during Catholic Mass Christ becomes miraculously present in the bread and wine, then the sacrifice is ongoing and continually necessary, enhancing the role of the Church and elevating it above scripture.

During the brief but significant reign of Edward VI a number of other important events and developments took place, which further strengthened the reformed movement. However, it is not possible to record all of them here. Suffice to say that among the highlights was the introduction of the Book of Common Prayer in 1549, followed by a revision in 1552.

Meanwhile, in 1550 Latimer suffered a period of severe ill-health during which he nearly died. Then having recovered, in 1551 he ceased to be the 'king's preacher',[5] and 'may be said to have again retired into private life.'[6] Unsurprisingly, he spent much of his time preaching in a variety of locations, including his native Leicestershire.

The young king, whose health had never been robust, became ill early in 1552, as measles and smallpox greatly weakened him. And by the turn of the year, 'fatal consumption had settled on him'.[7] Thus, on 6 July 1553 his death came as no surprise, although it was a tragic loss for adherents of the Reformation, as it appeared the substantial progress made might well be reversed. This was because the legitimate heir to the throne was Mary Tudor (appropriately named 'Bloody Mary'), who was a fanatical Catholic, desperate to see the tables turned on the reformers.

A desperate attempt was made to secure the throne for Lady Jane Grey (eldest granddaughter of the Duke of Suffolk), to keep Mary from occupying it, but this plot was in vain and sadly resulted in Lady Jane Grey's execution, who ever since has been tragically remembered as 'the nine days queen'.[8]

Chapter 10

Life under 'Bloody Mary'

From the moment Mary became Queen (in July 1553) Latimer knew his life was in grave danger. But unlike his encounter in chapter seven, this time he was settled in his mind and ready to pay the ultimate price as a Reformation preacher. However, we should not mistake this state of mind for anything approaching irrational fanaticism. On the contrary, as we have seen, 'he had always condemned any voluntary courting of martyrdom',[1] but now perhaps as never before in his life, he willingly accepted that 'a faithful man might have lawful cause for exposing himself to death.'[2]

Mary's 'reign of terror' posed a severe threat to the Reformation in England, not least because during this relatively short period (less than four years) nearly three hundred reformers were burnt at the stake for their biblical beliefs. And although Latimer had not behaved unlawfully in any way, 'he enjoyed too great a reputation among the common people to be left undisturbed.'[3] Preaching without concern for his safety in the Warwickshire area, he passively waited for an expected summons while other reformers fled (understandably) to the Continent to escape imprisonment and probable death.

Latimer was actually tipped off by a fellow reformer that a messenger was on his way, with orders to summon him to London. However, so calm and settled of mind was Latimer that instead of planning any escape, or even agonising as to what he should do next, he simply started to prepare for the long journey to London! Beside the astonishing bravery displayed, we should remember that Latimer was now an old man whose poor health would not easily withstand a long and arduous journey. And further, he knew that he was very unlikely to face anything approaching a fair trial on arrival in London, yet none of these factors deterred him.

When the messenger arrived he was astonished to be greeted warmly by Latimer who said to him:

> 'My friend, you be a welcome messenger to me. And be it known unto you, and to all the world, that I go as willingly to London at this present, being called by my prince to render a reckoning of my doctrine, as ever I was at any place in the world.'[4]

The messenger then left Latimer to make his way to London of his own accord. While this may sound very odd to a present day reader, especially when considering that Latimer represented a catch of national significance, there appears to have been a clear strategy in the messenger's actions. Latimer was almost certainly being given sufficient time and opportunity to escape! Thus, despite the hunger for his death, not least by Queen Mary, his enemies realised if he died honourably this might bolster the reformers' cause, while on the other hand, if he fled in fear, the fledgling Reformation movement would probably be fatally damaged. Needless to say Latimer had no second thoughts, but set out on the long journey without hesitation.

Not long after arriving in London, Latimer was summoned to appear before the Privy Council (the date in question being 13 September 1553).[5] Having surrendered his liberty for the sake of the gospel, Latimer was confined in the Tower immediately after the hearing, along with two other prominent reformers. One was Cranmer, the former Archbishop, the other Ridley, a younger but nonetheless experienced reformer. However, initially they were kept separately in solitary confinement. But even at this stage Latimer might still have escaped had he had the slightest inclination to do so. On 1 October Queen Mary's coronation took place and led to such a level of excitement that prisoner security was neglected.[6] However, such an opportunity did not weaken his resolve to remain in prison nor to bear witness to the God he had so faithfully served.

Despite their national significance, these three reformers were left to languish in their cells until March of the following year (1554).[7] During the winter, conditions were so bad that they would have proved 'unwholesome even to the most vigorous youthful frames',[8] and might well have proved fatal for Latimer and Cranmer in particular, had it not been for Latimer's forthright, if humorous exhortation to his jailer. He asserted that if conditions remained so bleak and cold, he would die in his cell, thus thwarting those who wanted to see him burn. His comments led to an improvement in their conditions but they were still kept separate until early in 1554, when in January the Tower suddenly filled with prisoners due to an unsuccessful revolt against the Queen. As a direct result, the three reformers were placed together in one cell, which enabled them to enjoy a brief period of fellowship, Bible study and prayer. Their time together lasted no longer than two months but it was precious and helped them to prepare for the ordeal ahead.

In March they were finally removed from their cell and sent to Oxford for the equivalent of a modern show trial (called officially, a disputation). On arrival they were locked in the town jail, the Bocardo. Their trial began on Saturday 14 April,[9] after which they were examined separately on 'three successive days'[10] from Monday to Wednesday of the following week. Latimer was tried last and though he was weak and frail he remained absolutely steadfast. In particular he robustly asserted that transubstantiation was just one of the Church of Rome's inventions with no basis in scripture.

Once the disputation was over the three men were once again kept separately. Intriguingly, Latimer was sent 'to the house of one of the bailiffs'[11] and not back to the town jail. Then on Friday 20 April they were summoned to be formally 'pronounced heretics and excommunicated'.[12] Latimer now expected to die imminently, however he (and Ridley) lived for another eighteen months! (Incidentally, Cranmer died separately and later still.) Throughout this period, though he was denied any direct access to his two dear brothers in the faith, he greatly encouraged them by sending messages of support and comfort. His own comfort came through further Bible reading and prayer, in which he engaged constantly.

In September 1555 Latimer and the other two reformers were given one last opportunity to recant but steadfast they remained, leading to the inevitable punishment of death by burning, and in the final chapter we shall focus on the harrowing but remarkable account of Latimer and Ridley dying together, for the sake of the Christian gospel and reformed faith. But to conclude this chapter it is worth pondering for a moment why the authorities tried once again to persuade the three reformers to recant. Quite probably they were aware that if these men could be either threatened or cajoled (both methods were used with Latimer) into a full recantation, the reformed movement would be severely weakened. At the same time, despite their hunger for the punishment of these distinguished leaders, the authorities risked being put to shame by the gracious and Christ-centred way in which they were preparing to face death. Martyrs senior in years and influence, quietly accepting such a cruel punishment, might well draw not only spectators but sympathisers who were increasingly convinced that the Church of Rome had indeed given itself up to evil practices and corruption. No doubt then, there was a degree of uneasiness among those who had pronounced sentence on these men, when the day of execution dawned.

Chapter 11

The preacher is martyred

As previously mentioned, Latimer and Ridley were put to death some time before Cranmer, thus on Wednesday 16 October 1555, two not three men were led out 'to the place of execution in a ditch near Balliol College'.[1] Ridley came first, and as he passed the Bocardo prison, he looked up in the hope of seeing Cranmer but he was busy in conversation with a friar and others, so they were unable to gesture a farewell to one another. But Ridley was not to be alone for much longer, as the following, intensely moving quotation reveals:

> 'Then Master Ridley looking back, espied Master Latimer coming after (from the bailiff's house), unto whom he said, "Oh be ye there?". "Yea", said Master Latimer, "have after as fast as I can follow;" so he, following a pretty way off, at length they came both to the stake, the one after the other, where first Dr. Ridley entering the place, marvellous earnestly holding up both his hands, looked towards heaven. Then, shortly after, espying Master Latimer, with a wondrous cheerful look he ran to him, embraced him and kissed him; and, as they that stood near reported, comforted him saying: "Be of good heart brother, for God will either assuage the fury of the flame or else strengthen us to abide it."[2]

More than one author has suggested that Latimer's comment ("have after as fast as I can follow") was a humorous one made at his own expense, as he was now elderly and infirm, hence the slow progress.[3] Further, as we have seen, he had always been quick witted and given to humorous remarks. However I dare to venture an alternative interpretation at this point. Latimer and Ridley had not seen each other since the disputation in April of the previous year, a period of eighteen months, therefore it must have been quite overwhelming for them to make contact, initially from a distance, and then face-to-face. But could it not also have been the case that Latimer was determined to be with his younger brother in the faith, to encourage him in their final hour of life together, and to assure him that he was not going to die alone. The sight and sound of these two men calling out to one another must have been deeply moving, and it is surely no wonder that their calm and quiet witness, when facing such an unjust and terrifying ordeal, led to an outpouring of grief among many spectators, and even the conversion of some from a religion of superstitious bondage to one of personal faith in Christ, in accordance with the scriptures.

Ridley and Latimer were then subjected to a sermon during which they were chastised and no doubt warned of the punishment to follow. Remarkably, the passage from which such sermons were preached was typically the Apostle Paul's first letter to the Corinthians and chapter 13, where the theme concerns the necessity of love in the Christian's life. Latimer and Ridley were no doubt reminded that if they surrender their bodies to the flames, but have not love, they gain nothing.[4] It appears that such preachers did not apply this passage of scripture to their own lives, otherwise they might have questioned the unjust ritual they were intimately involved in.

The sermon lasted only a quarter of an hour,[5] after which the two men were denied a request to speak, unless it was to recant. Both men then surrendered items of clothing (Ridley also giving away 'a few small mementos'[6]) before being 'chained to the stake, back to back'.[7] Ridley's brother then gave him (and subsequently Latimer too) some gunpowder in order to shorten the agony of the flames, which he gratefully received.[8] Then as the fire began to burn Latimer uttered words that have echoed down through the centuries:

'Be of good comfort Master Ridley, and play the man. We shall this day light such a candle, by God's grace, in England, as I trust shall never be put out.'[9]

Latimer died very quickly and possibly without pain, being 'overcome by the smoke'.[10] But in contrast, Ridley lingered for a long time, suffering terribly. The fire around him did not burn well, and as a direct result his legs were burnt while the flames failed to 'reach any of the vital parts.'[11] Eventually, the fire grew sufficiently intense for the gunpowder to explode, at which moment Ridley's life finally came to an end.

So much could be said at this point, but concerning Latimer, the concluding words of the great martyrologist, Foxe, are as appropriate as any:

'And thus much concerning this old and blessed servant of God, Master Latimer, for whose laborious travails, fruitful life, and constant death, the whole realm hath cause to give thanks to Almighty God.'[12]

Chapter 12

Latimer's legacy and our inheritance

When Latimer was born in the late 1400s, and for more than half his lifetime, the Church of Rome still appeared to have an iron grip on the country of England. Further, there were no obvious signs that all was about to change. To emphasise this significant fact, note the following quotation from an expert on England in the late middle ages:

'The Church had not yet lost any of its great wealth. It owned at least a fifth of the land of England and its treasures were still increasing in the early sixteenth century as men endowed, built, and adorned churches and chantries. And devotion to the Church manifested itself not only in gifts but in observances. Men still kissed the pax at Mass, still lit candles to their patron saints, still obtained indulgences for their sins, still went on pilgrimage, ----------. Parish churches were the centres of the social life of the community, and the clergy controlled education, hospitals, and poor relief. ---------- In short, the Church was everywhere in evidence and seemed to be all-powerful.'[1]

However, although Latimer died as a direct result of intense persecution toward the reformed movement, by the year of his death, much had changed. So much in fact, that another quotation (by another expert) aptly describes how the Reformation had taken hold and impacted both on parts of the Continent and England. (Note that while the book from which this quotation is taken focuses primarily on the Reformation in general rather than England specifically, it nevertheless helps to illustrate how the religious landscape of England changed dramatically during Latimer's lifetime.)

'The movement initiated by the renegade German friar Martin Luther brought an end to corrupt and oppressive rule by the clergy of an institutional Church, a Church that had maintained its power by imposing superstitious and psychologically burdensome beliefs on ordinary (lay) worshippers. It was also a return to the pure sources of Christianity, after centuries in which the stream was polluted by the dripping pipe of man-made traditions. The bible, the Word of God, was restored to its rightful place as the rule and arbiter of Christian life. In vernacular translations of scripture, lay readers met the person of Jesus Christ, bypassing the clerical mediators who, like officious secretaries, had kept medieval petitioners from direct contact with the boss.'[2]

The question for us to briefly discuss is to what extent did Latimer influence these events in England specifically? For the first forty years of his life his only influence was to maintain the status quo, but in the remaining thirty years everything changed.

Before reviewing Latimer's post-conversion influence we should pause for a moment to remember how unlikely a convert he was in the first place. Here was a man who had been born into a church-revering home that had no time for the heretical (and dangerous) teaching of the reformers. During his long period at Cambridge University he had also established his own credentials as one of the Church's champions, who was regarded as a reliable and dependable loyalist. And of course, in his own words he 'was as obstinate a papist as any was in England.'[3] But when the shy and quietly spoken Thomas Bilney entered his study in the spring of 1524, everything changed for Latimer. Consequently, great changes took place in England too!

Through Bilney, Latimer met the person of Jesus Christ as revealed in the pages of New Testament scripture, and realised his need not of superstitious rituals, but of life-giving repentance and faith towards God. This radical change inspired him to proclaim to all peoples the gospel of salvation by faith in Christ, and to boldly denounce the rituals of the Church that held so many in bondage. But critically, Latimer had a special gift whereby he could preach with equal effectiveness to the king and his court on the one hand, and the common people on the other. Thus when he left London for West Kington, he did not retire into obscurity, but continued to build his reputation as a preacher of national renown.

Though his partial recantation, when called before Convocation, was a sign of weakness (and probably of some ignorance too), he grew and matured as a reformer to enjoy widespread influence—as Bishop of Worcester especially—at a critical time for the Reformation movement. He also displayed extraordinary bravery when challenging and admonishing the king, whether concerning the need for the Bible in English for all to read or hear read aloud, or when chastening him for wrongful conduct.

But it is his words and conduct at the moment of death that perhaps have crystallised his legacy more than anything else, for at that point in history, he displayed a Christ-like spirit worthy of the name Christian, and emboldened Bible-believing Christians throughout England at a time when, humanly speaking, the Reformation could have melted away. His exhortation to Ridley just prior to being overcome by the flames and fumes of the fire, could be termed a final mini sermon,[4] not least because a far wider audience than those witnessing the spectacle on the day have been moved and influenced by it. Thus, just as Tyndale gave England the precious gift of the Bible in the language of common speech, Latimer complemented this seminal achievement by preaching and applying the written word, as God's unlikely instrument at a critical time, both in life and in death, to rich and poor alike.

Further reading

Alsop, James. *William Tyndale: An Introduction*
ELSP, 2009
I am more than a little embarrassed to be a self publicist, and am
certainly not making any kind of claim to have written a book of real
significance, however, as Latimer is often referred to as Tyndale's
complement, reading about the latter will help to piece together a fuller
history of the period. It will also introduce you to one of England's
greatest sons, not only on account of his contribution to the Reformation,
but the English language and its internationalisation. The book is of
identical size, format and price to this one.

Atherstone, Andrew. *The Martyrs of Mary Tudor*
Day One Publications, 2005
If you want to read a brief but informative account of what happened
to many Protestants under the violent reign of Mary Tudor ('Bloody
Mary') then this excellent book is hard to beat. The barbarity of death
by burning is laid bare, but so too the extraordinary testimony of Bible-
believing Christians from all walks of sixteenth century life.

Demaus, Rev. R. *Hugh Latimer: A Biography*
The Religious Tract Society, 1869
This is probably the most comprehensive and well written biography
of Hugh Latimer. Demaus had a superb gift for combining a fluent and
eloquent style with breathtaking thoroughness, and therefore nothing
since his work has been able to better it. My copy is an old original,
however you can now acquire a modern paperback edition from online
retailers (for example, The Book Depository), but it will not come cheap
despite the free postage and packing. Consider it a good investment for
a book of invaluable quality.

Loane, Marcus. *Masters of the English Reformation*
The Church Book Room Press, 1954
Combining brevity and detail with great skill, Loane introduces readers
to five individuals whose role in the early Reformation period was of
critical importance (Bilney, Tyndale, Latimer, Ridley and Cranmer).
This book is written in such a passionate, fast-flowing and arresting
style that it is hard to put down, and is likely to have a lasting impact
on anyone reading it with an open mind.

Marshall, Peter. *The Reformation. A Very Short Introduction*
Oxford University Press, 2009
For those wanting to understand the impact of the Reformation from
a Continental European perspective, this little book is a must. Written

by an expert with a flair (genius even) for conveying complex issues in a succinct manner, it is difficult to imagine a more accessible way to begin to understand this seminal period in European history, and its impact down through the centuries.

Wood, Douglas C. *Such a Candle. The Story of Hugh Latimer*
Evangelical Press, 1980
This superbly written account is the ideal next step for readers wanting to learn more about Latimer and his times. Drawing heavily on Demaus (as I have done) but also using a comprehensive range of sources throughout, it provides a concise but extremely thorough analysis of Latimer's life, character and work. Read alongside, before or after the Demaus biography, it will prove to be an indispensable aid.

Select Bibliography

Alsop, James. *William Tyndale: An Introduction*. ELSP, 2009

Atherstone, Andrew. *The Martyrs of Mary Tudor*. Day One Publications, 2005

Demaus, Rev. R. *Hugh Latimer: A Biography*. The Religious Tract Society, 1869

Duchars, Keith. *Saint Mary The Virgin*. West Kington. Published 1996 (Booklet—available from the church)

Foxe, John. *The Acts and Monuments of John Foxe*. Revised and Corrected by Rev. Josiah Pratt. The Religious Tract Society, [1877]

Houghton, S.M. *Sketches from Church History*. The Banner of Truth Trust, 1980

Jeffery, Peter. *Preachers who made a difference*. Evangelical Press, 2004

Loane, Marcus. *Masters of the English Reformation*. The Church Book Room Press, 1954

Marshall, Peter. *The Reformation. A Very Short Introduction*. Oxford University Press, 2009

Myers, A.R. *England in the Late Middle Ages*. Penguin Books Ltd, 1952

Stenton, Doris Mary. *English Society in the Early Middle Ages*. Penguin Books Ltd, 1951

Wood, Douglas C. *Such a Candle. The Story of High Latimer*. Evangelical Press, 1980

Abbreviations for sources specifically used and/or quoted from

Alsop. WT.	Alsop, James. *William Tyndale: An Introduction*. ELSP, 2009
Atherstone. MMT.	Atherstone, Andrew. *The Martyrs of Mary Tudor*. Day One Publications, 2005
Demaus. HL.	Demaus, Rev. R. *Hugh Latimer: A Biography*. The Religious Tract Society, 1869
Foxe. A&M.	Foxe, John. *The Acts and Monuments of John Foxe*. Revised and Corrected by Rev. Josiah Pratt. The Religious Tract Society, [1877]
Loane. MER.	Loane, Marcus. *Masters of the English Reformation*. The Church Book Room Press, 1954
Marshall. R.	Marshall, Peter. *The Reformation. A Very Short Introduction*. Oxford University Press, 2009

Myers. ELMA. Myers, A.R. *England in the Late Middle Ages.* Penguin Books Ltd, 1952

Wood. SC. Wood, Douglas C. *Such a Candle. The Story of High Latimer.* 1980

References and notes

Introduction
1 Myers. ELMA. Page 219

Chapter 1: Life and the Church in Latimer's times
1 Myers. ELMA. Page 205
2 The World Encyclopaedia. www. localhistories.org.children. 29/12/10
3 Demaus. HL. Page 5
4 As above. Page 45
5 When Latimer became parish priest of West Kington, his bishop was Cardinal Campeggio, who had never set foot in the diocese and only ever visited England once.

Chapter 2: Birth and early life
1 Demaus. HL. Page 6
2 As above. Page 8
3 As above. Page 30
4 Wood. SC. Page 8

Chapter 3: An unexpected conversion
1 Demaus. HL. Page 26
2 Foxe. A&M. Volume 4. Page 635
3 Demaus. HL. Page 37
4 Wood. SC. Page 10
5 Douglas Wood, in his excellent biography, often quoted from in this book, emphasises the significance of this complementary partnership on page 14.
6 Alsop. WT. Page 31
7 Wood. SC. Page 14

Chapter 4: Encountering Wolsey
1 Wood. SC. Page 15
2 As above. Page 16
3 As above. Page 18
4 As above. Page 19
5 Demaus. HL. Page 5
6 As above. Page 58

Chapter 5: Preaching before the King
1 Wood. SC. Page 42
2 Demaus. HL. Page 90
3 Wood. SC. Page 42
4 Alsop. WT. Page 57
5 Demaus. HL. Page 102
6 Wood. SC. Page 45
7 Demaus. HL. Page 104

Chapter 6: "To West Kington I will go"
1 Demaus. HL. Page 105
2 As above. Page 106
3 Wood. SC. Page 46
4 Demaus. HL. Page 109
5 As above. Page 110

Chapter 7: Dark clouds gather
1 Demaus. HL. Page 112
2 Wood. SC. Page 54
3 Demaus. HL. Page 120
4 Loane. MER. Page 41
5 Wood. SC. Page 56
6 Demaus. HL. Page 132
7 Wood. SC. Page 62
8 As above. Page 60
9 Demaus. HL. Page 134
10 Wood. SC. Page 60
11 Demaus. HL. Page 136
12 As above. Page 139
13 Wood. SC. Page 61
14 Demaus. HL. Page 143
15 As above.
16 As above. Page 143–144
17 Wood. SC. Page 63
18 Demaus. HL. Page 147
19 As above. Page 147–148

Chapter 8: Latimer the Bishop
1 Wood. SC. Page 64
2 As above.
3 One should not presume that

Cranmer had in any way positioned himself for this appointment, even though it filled other potential candidates with bitter envy. On the contrary, according to Loane. MER. it 'brought no joy to Cranmer; he could only regard it as a stern duty to which he must submit. As a husband with strong family affections, he would fear separation from his wife; as a scholar with strong literary habits, he would dread separation from his books. And all for the sake of a most imperious master in the person of King Henry VIII.' (See page 186.)

4 Wood. SC. Page 76
5 Demaus. HL. Page 172
6 Wood. SC. Page 78
7 As above. Page 86
8 Demaus. HL. Page 194
9 Foxe. A&M. Volume 7. Page 517
10 Wood. SC. Page 108
11 Alsop. WT. Page 56
12 Demaus. HL. Page 264
13 As above.
14 As above.
15 Wood.SC. Page 122
16 As above. Page 130
17 Demaus. HL. Page 340
18 As above. Page 339

Chapter 9: A new king reigns

1 Wood. SC. Page 147
2 Demaus. HL. Pages 396–397
Though I have quoted here from Demaus, see Loane. MER. Pages 128–129 for a longer quotation, set brilliantly in context. Of particular interest is Latimer's prior condemnation of inactive preachers and prelates who have neglected their parishioners' needs, choosing instead to concern themselves with their own success and status, in stark contrast to the Apostles.

3 It is important to emphasise that this biblical quotation means once for all time not once for everyone (see Romans 6:8–10).
4 See 1 Corinthians 10:16, which emphasises the spiritual union with Christ that takes place during the Communion Service.
5 Wood. SC. Page 158
6 Demaus. HL. Page 452
7 As above. Page 459
8 Atherstone. MMT. Page 11

Chapter 10: Life under 'Bloody Mary'

1 Demaus. HL. Page 470
2 As above.
3 Wood. SC. Page 160
4 Demaus. HL. Page 471
5 Wood. SC. Page 161
6 Demaus. HL. Page 474
7 Atherstone. MMT. Page 91
8 Demaus. HL. Page 473
9 Wood. SC. Page 164
10 Atherstone. MMT. Page 91
11 As above. Page 92
12 As above.

Chapter 11: The preacher is martyred

1 Atherstone. MMT. Page 97
2 Foxe. A&M. Volume 7. Page 548
3 Both Wood and Atherstone offer this explanation for Latimer's comment.
4 My reference here, to verse three, includes a plural adaptation.
5 Demaus. HL. Page 522
6 Atherstone. MMT. Page 98
7 As above.
8 Foxe. A&M. Volume 7. Page 550
9 As above.
10 Atherstone. MMT. Page 98
11 Demaus. HL. Page 523
12 Foxe. A&M. Volume 7. Page 550

Chapter 12: Latimer's legacy and our inheritance

1 Myers. ELMA. Pages 218–219
2 Marshall. R. Page 2
3 Wood. SC. Page 10
4 Interestingly, Loane. MER. describes this moment as one in which 'Latimer gave utterance to the noblest sermon he had ever composed.' Bearing in mind that Latimer was regarded as the greatest preacher of his day, Loane's comment further emphasises just how significant Latimer's words and conduct were, in these, the last few moments of his life. Nor is it surprising that his words of encouragement to Ridley have resonated with Bible-believing Christians down through the centuries. (See page 132.)

About the author

James Alsop is a teacher at Wiltshire College, where he lectures in tourism, politics and business. His main hobbies are reading and walking. Concerning the latter he has written three guidebooks, two of which (*The Mid-Wilts Way* and *Pewsey Rambles*) feature his home county of Wiltshire, while the third (*Walks on the Mendip Hills*) focuses on a compact region of Somerset, which in the author's view cannot be beaten for scenic quality and drama anywhere else in southern England. All three books are published by Ex Libris Press. He has also written a short introduction to William Tyndale (see further reading). He attends the Baptist Church in Bradford on Avon where he has been a member for more than twenty-eight years. He is married to Kate and they have two daughters, Evangeline and Isabella.

  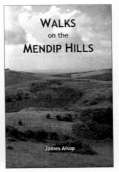

Walking guides by James Alsop, Published by Ex Libris Press, each £5.95